This book is dedicated to all who find Nature not an adversary to conquer and destroy, but a storehouse of infinite knowledge and experience linking man to all things past and present. They know conserving the natural environment is essential to our future well-being.

HALEAKALĀ
THE STORY BEHIND THE SCENERY®

by Jim Mack

Jim Mack is a career professional with the National Park Service. Since receiving his degree in wildlife management from California State University at Humboldt, Jim has spent many years in the interpretive program of the Park Service, including his assignment as interpretive specialist at Hawai'i's Haleakalā National Park.

Captions by Linda Moore, Seasonal Park Interpreter.

***Haleakalā National Park,** located on the island of Maui, Hawai'i, was established in 1916 to preserve a scenic volcano and the fragile ecosystem of Kīpahulu Valley.*

Front cover: Haleakalā Crater from the visitor center, photo by Jeff Gnass. Inside front cover: 'Ohe'o Gulch and Kīpahulu Valley from Kūloa Point, photo by Larry Ulrich. Page 1: Nēnē goose, photo by Greg Vaughn. Pages 2/3: Clouds linger in Haleakalā Crater, photo by Jeff Gnass.

Edited by Mary L. Van Camp. Book design by K. C. DenDooven.

Eighth Printing, 2002 • Revised Edition

LC 92-70431. ISBN 0-88714-052-1.

The road draws us on, brief glimpses of the mountain's interior tease our curiosity. Rising higher we imagine other climbers from other times: the ancient Hawaiians treading in sandalled feet, the early explorers on horseback. Breaking through the clouds we find ourselves perched at the top of the world, on the summit of Haleakalā

CARL SHANEFF

Early one day, long before sunrise, Māui, the mischievous demigod known throughout the Pacific Islands, crept to the summit of Haleakalā where he lay waiting for the sun's first spidery legs to appear. As they came over the edge of the volcano's rim one by one, he lassoed each ray and secured it to a wiliwili tree. The sun, now unable to move, begged for its freedom. But Māui would not release the sun until it had promised to slow its daily rush across to the sky so that Māui's mother could finish her daily chores of drying kapa cloth and preparing food while there was yet daylight. Māui left some of the ropes attached to the sun to remind it of its promise to travel more slowly across the heavens. Every evening, just before the sun sets, the ropes can be seen trailing off into the night sky as daylight fades.

This is the story, from a distant but not forgotten time, of how the early Hawaiians came to call the mountain, on the island of Maui, *Haleakalā*, House of the Sun."

Haleakalā has influenced the lives of people from the time they first beheld its massiveness. The story of its creation and development is as interesting and rich as any of the legends of old Hawai'i. Wind, water, and fire joined forces to create the volcano of Haleakalā. When we stand on its summit and gaze down into its heart, we have the feeling of having entered another world, a world in which the moonlike landscape, rolling downward and off into the

Beyond the vast basin atop Haleakalā, above the clouds, loom the great peaks of Mauna Kea and Mauna Loa on the Big Island of Hawai'i. Younger than those that form Maui, these volcanoes have both been active in modern times.

distant fog-cloaked rim, seems to beckon hypnotically with its desolate beauty.

Few parks offer a cross-section of nature's handiwork as rich and varied as Haleakalā. In its incomparable vistas of multi-hued cinder cones; barren, windswept summits; cascading pools of water; and lush, green, semitropical forests, Haleakalā provides an experience unique and refreshing, perhaps even euphoric.

For there is a kind of magic here. You can see it in the afternoon shadows that creep across the valley floor and in the last flaming brush of sunset that tinges the clouds gold, pink, and orange. You can hear it in the soft, almost human sigh of the nēnē, the native goose that lives along the vegetated slopes in the immense valley. And you can feel it everywhere.

In this land of sky and clouds and crimson craters, Haleakalā is truly the most sublime volcanic spectacle in the world. To stand upon its rim is an exhilarating experience from which memory may draw for a lifetime.

A Timeless Panorama

Haleakalā's valley, formed by the processes of volcanism and erosion, is actually the 3,000-foot (900 km) deep summit depression of a volcano that has not erupted since 1790. Huge as it is—7.5 miles (12 km) across and 2.5 miles (4 km) wide—and splashed with vivid colors and contrasts, it is often compared in scenic grandeur to the Grand Canyon. The comparison is more than superficial; like the huge gorge in Arizona, the 19-square-mile (49 sq km) area of the valley was formed largely by the action of water. Lying near the southeastern end of the Hawaiian archipelago, Haleakalā represents an intermediate stage in a complex, conveyor-belt process that builds and then destroys the islands that make up the mid-Pacific chain.

One of the basic concepts underlying the process of the creation of the Hawaiian chain is the *plate tectonics* theory which considers the surface of the earth to be made up of more than a dozen relatively thin, rigid plates that cover the earth like the cracked shell of an egg and "float" on the *mantle*, a more-or-less fluid layer of very hot rock. Scientists theorize that thermal convection within the mantle causes these plates to remain in slow but constant motion all over the surface of the earth.

Visitors to the Kīpahulu coast of Maui witness the dynamic interplay of richly textured volcanic cliffs, vibrant waters, and ever-shifting light.

The direction of plate movement is predictable and can be measured. For example, the Pacific plate, on which the islands of Hawai'i are situated, is moving northwesterly toward Japan at the rate of 3-5 inches (7-13 cm) each year. Most of the plates covering the earth move in different directions relative to each other. As a result adjoining plates are sometimes forced over or under one another, causing uplift and submergence. Occasionally they just barely slide past each other, and the resulting jerky movement causes earthquakes along the junction. The earthquakes that occasionally rumble through California are the results of just this kind of movement—in these cases, the sliding of the Pacific plate against the North American plate, sometimes along the San Andreas fault. Increased volcanic activity is usually present along these seams in the crust of the earth. The perimeter of the Pacific plate, at the edge of the Pacific Ocean Basin, is no exception. It is called the ring of fire because its outline traces a circle of active or recently active volcanoes.

The Hawaiian Islands, however, were formed in a different manner. Located instead in the *middle* of the Pacific plate, they were formed as the result of the movement of the plate over a hot spot in the earth's mantle. Lava welling out upon the ocean floor for millions of years gradually built the islands one by one, a process that is still going on. As one island moves away from the influence of the hot spot, another island be-

Born on the floor of the ocean and rising, layer upon thin layer, Haleakalā once stood nearly three thousand feet taller than it does today.

gins to form on the ocean floor. The depth of the ocean is so great that most of the mass of each island (each volcanic mountain) lies hidden far below the surface of the water. The Hawaiian Islands, then, are actually the very peaks of a long underwater mountain range that is permanently anchored to the continuously moving Pacific plate. Haleakalā itself rises to a height of 10,023 feet (3,055 m) above the surface of the ocean. Below it the mountain descends for another 19,000 feet (5,791 m) to the ocean floor.

Once these moving islands have shifted away from the influence of the hot spot, the forces of erosion begin to predominate. Rain cascading down the mountainous slopes gradually erodes the volcanic islands and carries the eroded material back to the sea. Maui, the second youngest island and still not completely out of the influence of the hot spot, has nevertheless started on an erosional journey that will end only when the island is returned to the sea from which it emerged. Maui's slopes still appear relatively youthful, but they will one day—like Kaua'i, its older neighbor to the northwest—bear the scars of deep canyons.

Each of the innumerable twists and turns of the serpentine road to Hāna reveals something new to those willing to make this slow and bumpy drive. As the road winds its way along Maui's northeastern coast it snakes through dark, cool stands of vegetation and balances atop sheerly dropping cliffs; offering glimpses of white waterfalls, blue ocean, and the steep, green slopes of Haleakalā.

Honomanū Volcanic Period

Haleakalā's geologic history has been divided into three periods of activity. The initial building period, *Honomanū*, is estimated to have begun about a million or so years ago, around the time that the woolly mammoth and the saber-toothed tiger roamed the face of the earth. Haleakalā's birth began deep on the ocean floor. Its conception was uneventful, and the surface of the restless ocean revealed little of the volcanic activity far below. This quiet building process continued for thousands and thousands of years. Tremendous pressures at these great depths and the relatively low volumes of gas contained in the magma (molten rock) caused the lava flows to form thin, wide-spreading layers. Gradually the mountain neared the surface, and as it did the character of the eruption changed. No longer at great depths and under the burden of the pressure of water, super-heated lava came into contact with shallower waters and caused giant explosions of steam, rock, and ash. Billowing, ash-laden clouds towering thousands of feet into the air proclaimed the presence of a new volcano and a new island in the Hawaiian chain.

Once the volcanic peak was safely out of the reach of the waves, lava continued to pour downslope from the summit vents, and the mountain grew steadily toward the sky. It wasn't until Haleakalā's summit was several thousand feet above sea level that its repeated outpourings of lava washed up against the much older Pu'u Kukui (West Maui), forming the isthmus connecting Maui's two volcanic peaks. Since that time, surface runoff has washed additional material down from both mountains to spread a rich layer of alluvium over the older lava flows. The isthmus today is about 7 miles (11 km) across and at one point reaches approximately 200 feet (60 m) above sea level.

Honomanū lavas make up the foundation for all of East Maui. They can be seen on the northern

coast, particularly along the sea cliffs just west of the town of Ke'anae. At the conclusion of the Honomanū period the elevation of Haleakalā was about 8,500 feet (2,600 m) above the present sea level. It is not known whether a caldera (a volcano whose summit has collapsed) ever formed on the summit during this period, since there is no evidence remaining. The volcano probably was simi-
ance to the relatively youthful
Hawai'i) of today.
ne the island of Maui was much
, it included six major volcanic
sts call this prehistoric island *Maui*
"). It included the present-day is-
Moloka'i, Lana'i, and Kaho'olawe.
is only about half the size of the
and of Hawai'i (the Big Island),
n area of 2,000 square miles (5,180
' Maui covers 729 square miles
Lower sea levels, caused by the
arge amounts of water in frozen
eologically recent past, uncovered
at once joined these four islands.
other ice age could lower the sea
that the land connecting these is-
in become visible and the island
ıld be reborn.

Kula Volcanic Period

The second of the three volcanic series associated with the building of Haleakalā is the *Kula* series. The sources of lava for this stage of growth were located along several fissures, known as *rift zones* . From the summit of Haleakalā three rift zones have been identified: one trending north, the second east, and the third southwest. Lava may have issued from any one, two, or all three rift zones at the same time. Practically the entire present summit of Haleakalā Volcano is comprised of Kula-period lavas. They are visible in the road cuts within the park, and hikers can see them along the west *pali* (cliff) on the Halemau'u trail. They form a dense, relatively continuous sheet of lava that is 2,000 feet (600 m) thick near the summit. Soil formations between the layers of lava indicate that the volcano was quiet for long periods of time between eruptions.

The Kula period was probably the most spectacular of the volcanic series. It was marked by large, occasionally explosive displays of volcanic activity in which cinder cones of various sizes were formed. Cross sections of the numerous Kula-period cinder cones are exposed in several places along the Kalahaku pali. Subsequent erosion has also exposed the remnants of numer-

of
is
's
h
a
st
k
k
f
.
"

JEFF GNASS

CARL SHANEFF

Less resistant to the powerful forces of time than these dense basalt dikes are the fragile archaeological sites also scattered among the cliffs of Haleakalā. The park is charged with protecting these as well as its abundant natural resources.

ous volcanic dikes and plugs along this same *pali.* Dike formations are the dense, erosion-resistant remains of the lava that forced its way up in zigzag fashion through vertical cracks and crevices in older lava layers. These intrusive formations are usually less than 10 feet (3 m) wide and are composed of fine-grained basalt. Fragments from these dikes were valued by early Hawaiians for the production of stone adzes. Many quarry sites have been found, especially at the more accessible formations. The adze, chipped to the proper shape by a hammerstone and then secured to a wooden handle, was an important tool of the Hawaiians, since it was used for a multitude of jobs.

Several lava dikes may be found in one locality. Known as dike *swarms*, these are often sites of large quantities of groundwater, for as rainwater percolates through porous layers of ash and cinders, it is channeled by these vertical dike formations and accumulates, forming springs and seeps along crater walls.

When intrusive flows are wider and terminate in large, mushroom-shaped formations, they are called plugs. A large concentration of plugs is not unusual near the summit throat of a volcano, and Haleakalā has such an accumulation near the western end of its valley, about 1.25 miles (2 km) east of what is now the summit. Combining this information with the angle of the outer slopes, geologists theorize that at the conclusion of the Kula-period eruptions the summit of Haleakalā was probably at least 3,000 feet (900 m) higher and farther east than it is today.

The Kula period was responsible for a major portion of the building of Haleakalā. It also witnessed the carving of its spectacular valley and, in its declining years, increasingly longer intervals of inactivity. During these periods the battle between the forces of erosion and volcanic activity was continuous. Valleys cut by stream erosion often were refilled by lava pouring down the newly cut stream channels. Gradually the less spectacular forces of erosion began to win the contest, etching ever-deepening valleys into the slopes of Haleakalā. Torrential rains brought by prevailing northeast trade winds cut deeper into the north-facing Ke'anae Valley and to a lesser extent the Kaupō Valley, eventually merging to produce the vast depression at the summit. At the conclusion of the Kula period, the sides of the two great water-carved gaps formed the walls of Haleakalā Volcano. Today, the gaps in the volcano rim and the valleys below present excellent illustrations of the power of the forces of erosion.

Like most Hawaiian valleys, these two major gorges were formed with amphitheater-shaped heads and narrow stream channels, traits resulting from the feeding of a fan of many tributaries into the headwaters of a valley. This formation captured many small streams and accelerated the rate and scope of erosion. Waterfalls developed as the valleys carved their way toward the summit, and these cascading streams accelerated the carving process.

Although it appears forbidding and barren seen from its rim, Haleakalā Wilderness Area provides sheltered niches for many plants and animals. Campers at Paliku, at the head of Kaupō Gap are likely to see nēnē wading through the meadow and birds such as the 'apapane and 'i'iwi flitting among the native 'ohia and mamane trees.

The probable reason for the largeness of the valley is that the two valleys did not meet at the exact summit but were offset to one side of each other, forming a large elbow. Greater erosional progress was made by the Ke'anae Valley because of the large amounts of loose cinder material along its rift zone and because of the abundant rainfall it received. The remains of the wall that once separated the two valleys can be seen near the center of the erosional depression as a weathered ridge line extending from Hanakauhi peak in a southerly direction. The erosional process has not stopped; a similar escarpment separates the valley depression from Kīpahulu Valley. Someday this too will erode through, forming yet another gap.

During this time, Haleakalā was gradually aging and probably resembled the present cone-studded volcano Mauna Kea, on the island of Hawai'i. After the quiet conclusion of the Kula period, the volcano became active again, entering its third and perhaps final period of activity.

ED COOPER

Clouds are drawn into the park up Ko'olau Gap, providing cooling moisture and cloaking the land. For centuries the summit's wealth and mysteries have drawn people in as well. The earliest visitors to the summit area came to hunt, to gather, and to practice their religion. Today we come to see, to experience, and to learn.

PETER FRENCH

The volcano at Haleakalā has now awakened since Europeans began keeping a written account of its history. The date 1790 for Maui's last lava flow is the result of comparisons made between the navigational charts mapped of the island in 1786 and in 1793.

Hāna Volcanic Period

The Hāna period, the last major activity phase of Haleakalā Volcano, is estimated to have ended 800 to 1,000 years ago. Almost all the colorful cinder cones along the east-rift zone inside the valley are the result of Hāna-period activity, which was characterized by explosive (and probably very spectacular) fire fountains. As the material from these eruptions fell back around the vent, it formed these large cones of cinders. The biggest of all, Pu'uo Maui (Hill of Maui), is nearly 1,000 feet (300 m) high. The dark lava flow that extends to the northeast from the base of Kamoali'i cinder cone was also a product of this period.

Hāna-period lava flows issuing from the east-rift zone followed the path of least resistance down the Ke'anae and Kaupō valleys and rushed toward the ocean. It is estimated that the accumulated depths of these last flows may be as great as 3,000 feet (900 m) in some places. Hāna lavas were frequently thin and very fluid. As the molten rock raced down the valleys and depressions, it often left a thin veneer of lava, sometimes only inches thick, which adhered to the valley walls. Flows of mud triggered by the lava created broad plains below the mouth of Kaupō Gap.

Along the volcano's slopes, windblown ash and cinders remain, testifying to the volcanic activity that occurred here and to the tremendous volume of volcanic material that was thrown into

The lava flows offer an environment with challenges such as extremely porous soil, intense sunlight, freezing temperatures, and low rainfall that native plants like the kupaoa are uniquely adapted to meet.

the air during eruptions. The heavy accumulation of such materials on the western side indicates that the prevailing winds at the time of the eruption were from the east.

In 1978, Dr. Gordon A. Macdonald, U.S. Geological Survey, analyzed a sample of carbonized tree found buried along the upper east-rift zone near the headwaters of Kīpahulu Valley. The living tree was engulfed by volcanic activity approximately 9,300 years ago, according to the carbon-14 data. It is not known whether there have been subsequent eruptions in this section of the park, but it is likely.

The most recent chapter in the volcanic history of Haleakalā occurred outside the park along the southwest-rift zone in an area now known as La Perouse Bay. There, in about 1790, lava from two up-slope vents poured down the flank of the volcano and into the ocean, forming a peninsula. Because of the recency of this lava flow (when compared to the age of the entire mountain), geologists classify Haleakalā as an *active* volcano. The frozen, jagged surface of this flow is a mute reminder of the possibility that Haleakalā may erupt again.

Among the most interesting products of explosive volcanic activity are volcanic *bombs*, found in a wide variety of sizes. Formed when fragments of molten lava were forcefully flung from an eruption vent, they are commonly associated with cinder-cone formation. As the molten fragments flew through the air, they often cooled before striking the ground and thus retained their shapes, which are unique and highly variable—from the "spindle bomb," which has a projection at one or both ends, to the "cow-dung bomb," which resulted when lava that was only partially cooled hit the ground. They are also found in a wide variety of sizes, from those that can be held in the palm of the hand to giants that weigh several tons.

There are other geologic phenomena amid the cinder cones dotting the valley floor that are just as fascinating. Among these phenomena are *lava tubes*, caves formed when the surface of a

ED COOPER

Geologists have adopted the descriptive Hawaiian terms "aa," meaning rough, and "pahoehoe," meaning smooth, to distinguish between the two types of lava flows. Although hundreds of years have passed since lava last flowed through the valley at Haleakalā, the jumbled, rough appearance of the aa flows lead many to believe that Pele laid them down only yesterday.

Many traditional Hawaiian stories and chants recount the adventures of Pele, the powerful and temperamental goddess of volcanoes and fire. The travels, battles, and love affairs described in these tales are played out on the Hawaiian landscape; and many landmarks throughout the Islands have names that refer to these events. To spend the day walking the trails at Haleakalā is to be surrounded by the places, moods, and colors described in these tales. Especially colorful is the area known as "Pele's Paintpot." The spectrum of colors one sees here reflects the variety of minerals present in the lava.

LARRY ULRICH

narrow flow of lava cools and solidifies while the inside remains viscous and continues to move, eventually draining out and leaving a hollow tube. Some tubes are quite small, and their collapsed remains can be seen as dome-shaped rubble heaps on the surface. Others are large enough to accommodate a person standing upright, but because there is always a danger of collapse, and because ancient burials occur in some tubes, the Park Service cautions visitors against entering caves for their own safety and the protection of cultural resources.

In the central valley area, Ka Pā Pua'ao Pele ("Pele's Pig Pen"), a small spatter vent, resembles a holding pen for livestock. It was named in recognition of its legendary owner, Madame Pele, the Hawaiian volcano goddess whose fiery activity created the volcanic islands of Hawai'i. Kawilinau ("Bottomless Pit"), plunging 60 or 70 feet (18 or 20 meters) straight down, is also located near the center of the valley. Kawilinau is believed to be the place where Pele's sister Kamakokahai, goddess of the surface of the sea, attempted to force her way into the valley in order to destroy Pele's fires. "Pele's Paint Pot" is yet another feature named for the goddess; it owes the beauty of its chaotic splashes of rich color to the various by-products of volcanic activity. Yellows come from sulphur deposits, and the various shades of red result from oxidation of iron.

The search for patterns and colors should not stop with the largest and most easily recognized features; there are also surprises on a very small scale. Closer examination of various volcanic rocks reveals mineral crystals that sparkle and shine when held in the sun. Olivine and augite—glassy, lustrous crystals of green and black respectively—are the most conspicuous of these.

The valley floor abounds with other evidences of Pele's artistic talent. Lava in the form of pyramids, squeeze-ups, and delightful twists resembling candy taffy are intriguing displays that stimulate the imagination. At the same time, they evoke astonishment at the versatility of forces great enough to build mountains yet delicate enough to carve jewels.

SUGGESTED READING

MACDONALD, GORDON A., and AGATIN T. ABBOTT. *Volcanoes in the Sea.* Honolulu: University of Hawaii Press, 1983.

MACDONALD, GORDON and DOUGLASS HUBBARD. *Volcanoes of the National Parks of Hawai`i.* Honolulu: Hawai`i Natural History Association, 1989.

TILLING, ROBERT, CHRISTINA HELIKER, and THOMAS WRIGHT. *Eruptions of Hawaiian Volcanoes: Past, Present and Future.* Denver, Colorado: U.S. Geological Survey, 1987.

Preserving the Unique

The development of life on the volcanic islands that are emerging from the sea, such as the Hawaiian Islands, echoes events that occurred millions of years ago in the time-shrouded history of the earth. These islands constitute unusual biological "laboratories" where certain species of plants and animals hardy enough to traverse thousands of miles of open ocean were able to gain a foothold in a fresh new environment with little, if any, competition from other life forms.

The odds against terrestrial life finding the way to such isolated, insular environments as Hawai'i are overwhelming. Over two thousand miles lie between these islands and the nearest continental land mass. Biologists calculate that the present native flora is the result of the successful immigration of only one new plant species every 40,000 years!

For those few species that survived the journey and adapted to the new environment, the isolation of Hawai'i has proved to be a blessing in disguise. The qualities that have come to be associated with Hawaiian flora and fauna in fact *depended* upon this isolation. The ocean was not only a highly selective barrier but it was an effective insulator as well. Hawai'i's life forms, acting together over a vast amount of time, were thus able to evolve into a variety of previously unknown and very unusual forms.

Over the years since the arrival of people, this unique "biology" has given way to human needs, and havens for the native flora and fauna of old Hawai'i have become fewer and fewer. Today the mountain tops are among the last outposts for the beleaguered remnants of a natural experiment in evolution, a biological "game of chance." Thus, one of the primary reasons for the existence of Haleakalā National Park, which occupies the summit of East Maui and a pristine valley on its southeastern flank, is to preserve a large portion of a biota that is uniquely Hawaiian.

In discussing Hawaiian plants and animals, several terms commonly used must be understood: The term native is applied to any plant or

GREG VAUGHN

Curious visitors come to Haleakalā hoping to see the equally curious Hawai'i an goose, the nēnē, found today only here and on the Big Island of Hawai'i.

The silvery glow of the silverswords, created by tiny reflective hairs that cover their leaves, ma[illegible] them beacons shining out of the valley's dep[illegible]

animal that reached the area where it now grows without the help of people. *Alien* species, on the other hand, arrived with the aid of people (via either the early Polynesian voyagers or subsequent arrivals). Among native species, there are *endemic* organisms, native to only a small geographic area (such as the silversword, a plant found only in Hawai'i), and *indigenous* life forms, native to a larger geographic area (such as the *'ohi 'a lehua*, a plant found in all of Polynesia and New Zealand.

Development Of Life

Plants whose seeds can be transported by winds are the best candidates for migration to an island. Consequently ferns, whose spores are extremely light, are well represented in Hawai'i with 168 native species. Large plants too can have light seeds. The seeds of the *'ohi'a lehua* can drift on winds of less than six miles per hour.

Plants frequented by birds are also good prospects for long-distance dispersal. Many plant seeds, eaten and retained in digestive tracts of birds or attached externally to their feathers or feet, have made the long journey to the Islands. The American golden plover, a migratory shorebird that winters in Hawai'i, may well be responsible for the introduction of plants that occur both in this bird's arctic breeding grounds and in the high-elevation grasslands within Haleakalā National Park.

Contrary to what may be a popular conception, ocean flotation of seeds to the Hawaiian Islands accounts for only a very few introductions; there aren't many seeds capable of withstanding the harsh ocean conditions for extended periods. Two notable exceptions, the koa and wiliwili trees, are found in the area of the park. Seeds from the ancestors of these two trees may have floated to the shores of Maui from other islands in the chain, or perhaps from Australia or other islands far to the southwest. Wiliwili can still be seen in remnant dry forest on Maui's southern coast; the best place to see koa is in lower Kaupō Gap.

JOHN I. KJARGAARO

Lobelias favor the moist climate of their native Hawai'i. Several native birds have evolved beaks that are shaped to correspond with the shape of this or other native flowers, enabling them to gather nectar specifically from these plants. The survival of bird and flower may rest on this interdependency, illustrating how important it is to preserve whole ecosystems rather than just isolated species.

Hikers wishing to experience the entire range of Haleakalā's diversity can make a trip from the cinder desert near the park's summit, through the varying terrain of the Haleakalā Wilderness Area, then down to the ocean through Maui's grasslands on the steep Kaupō trail.

For island animal life, the odds against making the migration by ocean proved to be at least as great as for plants. Only two mammals succeeded in making the hazardous journey to Hawai'i—the monk seal and the Hawaiian bat. The latter, though not frequently seen, is among the inhabitants of the park.

Hawaiian birds are a spectacular success story. About 15 kinds of avian immigrants gave rise to about 70 species of historically known Hawaiian birds. In addition, fossils of many extinct species continue to be uncovered by researchers from the Smithsonian Institution. The unique subfamily of Hawaiian honeycreepers is the world's most diverse group of birds regarding eating habits and bill structure. Within this group are such different birds as the *'akialoa*, whose beak is adapted to feeding on the delicate long-necked lobelia flowers, and the Maui parrotbill, whose massive beak structure enables it to break twigs to locate its food.

Living primarily at the eastern end of Haleakalā Volcano, near Palikū, is the Hawaiian goose, or *nēnē*. Although it is believed to have evolved from the Canada goose, it has gradually developed into a distinct species.

The bird was once exterminated from Maui, but through the cooperative efforts of the State Department of Fish and Game, the Wildfowl and Wetlands trust in England, and the National Park Service, its population was reestablished in Haleakalā Volcano during the 1960s. The nēnē, which only forty years ago numbered less than fifty in the wild, is also found on the island of Hawai'i. It was there, in fact, that the initial international effort to save the species from extinction began.

Hawai'i's insects must take first prize for successful establishment and great diversity. From roughly 300 original immigrants, they have expanded into over 7,000 different species, and more are being identified each year. This insect world is inhabited by a beautiful collection of nature's finest and tiniest handiwork. For Haleakalā the number and variety of its small denizens are still being calculated, but initial discoveries have been exciting and unusual. We can only hope there is time enough to discover the unknown members of this fascinating world before critical balances in their life cycles are upset by inadvertent changes in their environment.

Successful migration is but half the story of colonizing an island world. We will never know the number of immigrants that—for lack of a specific pollinating insect, or a male or female member of the species, or the necessary conditions for seed germination, or a food source—were unable to reproduce after having completed the incredible journey.

Faced with a wide variety of fresh habitats, the successful colonizers adapted in different ways to the new environment. Eventually these species differentiated enough to become almost unrecognizable when compared with their ancestors. Biologists continue to study Hawaiian species as textbook products of evolutionary processes. The great diversity found in species occurring at sea level as well as on mountain tops and forests led early scientists to erroneously believe they had discovered many new species. Further study revealed that some of the supposedly distinct species were actually many different forms of only one type. Some of the plant species possessed the remarkable ability to change leaf size, overall shape, or degree of hairiness to enable them to cope with the changing environmental conditions in the vertical geography of the islands. Thus the pukiawe and the 'ohi 'alehua found in dry-forest conditions varied considerably from those found in rain-forest habitats.

The absence here of large grazing animals and predators—because of their inability to cross the ocean barrier—has significantly influenced the development of island flora and fauna. No longer required to ensure their survival through protective measures, almost all of Hawai'i's plants are without thorns, offensive odors, and toxic substances. The thornless *'akala* (raspberry) and odorless mint are but two examples in Haleakalā.

Mutations among birds have resulted in flightlessness—a development that would have been an evolutionary dead-end in an environment in which they would have been preyed upon by ground-dwelling animals. Fossils of a flightless ibis, a bird now extinct from unknown causes, were recently discovered near Haleakalā and in other locations in the Hawaiian chain. At least four species of flightless geese shared pre-

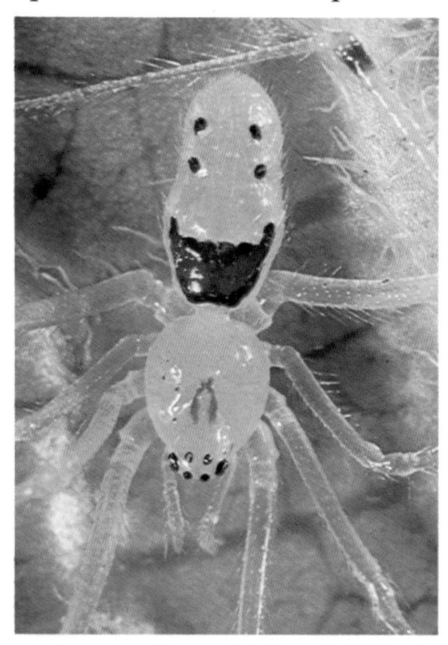

The immense task of inventorying the insects of the park, not to mention all of Hawai'i, is far from complete. This fascinating array is a constant source of discovery. How many other species may have been lost through the careless disruption of their habitat?

PHOTOS BY W.P. MULL

Hawai'i's cultural history is closely linked to its rich natural heritage. The wood of the koa tree, which once grew in vast forests along Haleakalā's outer slopes, was shaped into the outrigger canoes and surfboards characteristic of this culture. The native people of Hawai'i surrounded this highly prized tree with spiritual significance and protected it from overuse with strict religious taboos. Today the wood of the koa is still highly valued for its deep color and beautiful grain. This popularity, coupled with the clearing of the land for agricultural uses, has reduced the vast koa forests to scattered stands.

JOHN I. KJARGAARD

historic Maui with the *nēnē*. Today only the *nēnē*, still a capable flier, remains.

One of the most interesting of the processes by which species evolve into different forms is *neoteny*, in which certain characteristics normally associated with the juvenile stages are retained in the adult stage. Some biologists think that the mature silversword plant evolved through the process of neoteny from a group of plants called "tarweeds." This group of plants, found along the coastal areas of North and Central America, has a juvenile developmental stage that closely resembles the mature silversword. It is not inconceivable that the tarweed, like the silversword a member of the sunflower family, arrived attached to the feathers or feet of a migrating bird and eventually developed into the silversword, a form capable of surviving on Haleakalā's barren slopes.

Life Zones

Although plants and animals are often very adaptable, they are limited by the types of conditions under which they can survive. The fact that certain communities of plants are found at specific elevations or in areas of high or low rainfall is not accidental. Each species has its own set of environmental conditions outside which it does not naturally exist. These communities of plants and their associated interdependent animals are called *life zones.* Generally altitudinal and latitudinal in nature, they change as one drives north or south on large continents or up and down on large mountains. One of the pleasures of visiting mountainous areas is being able to observe the differing life zones that have developed as a result of the major factors of temperature, moisture, soil, and sunlight. In ascending the leeward side of Haleakalā from sea level to the summit, over 10,000 feet (3,000 m) above, there is a rough equivalency to the life zones one would encounter in driving north to Alaska from the latitude of central Mexico. As environmental conditions change, so do the plant and animal life.

Ascending the slopes of Haleakalā, the temperature drops about three degrees Fahrenheit per 1,000 feet (one degree Celcius per 174 meters) in elevation. This drop is fairly gradual until the temperature-inversion layer between 5,000 and 7,000 feet (1,500 and 2,000 m) is reached. This inversion, formed by heat rising from the surrounding land mass, eventually cools and forms a lid that traps the warm, moist air below. The moisture-laden trade winds come into contact with the high-elevation cool air and cause moisture to precipitate out in the form of either clouds or rain. The inversion layer is responsible for the fact that a wreath of clouds often gently hugs Haleakalā's slopes although clear skies prevail above and below the summit. Above the inversion layer, the temperature decreases at the same rate that it did below it.

The inversion layer plays a very important role in the development of plant communities on the slopes of Haleakalā. Very little moisture falls above the inversion; consequently vegetation gets sparser as one proceeds farther up the mountain. At the summit the landscape is almost a desert, largely devoid of plant life.

The park has four native life zones. The largest accessible group of plants is the shrub community, which covers the outer western slopes of the park between 7,000 and 9,000 feet (2,100 and 2,700 m) in elevation. The switchbacks on the road to the summit weave through a low-lying brushfield of *'ōhelo, pukiawe, hinahina* (silver geranium), and bracken fern. This shrub community is located just above the inversion layer and consequently receives little rainfall. Clouds frequently sweep across this face of the mountain, and most of the plants have developed special features—such as reduced leaf sizes, hairy surfaces, and dense growth patterns—to help them trap windborne moisture, prevent excessive evaporation, and reduce exposure to the intense ultraviolet rays received at these high elevations.

The orange-colored fruits of the pilo attract attention to this common shrub.

The sandalwood tree, highly prized for its beautiful and fragrant heartwood, was harvested so extensively that it has disappeared from the lower elevations of the island.

Scattered sandalwood trees, or *'iliahi,* are also found in this life zone. Once occurring at lower elevations in the dry-forest areas, this tree was exploited for its fragrant heartwood, which the Chinese used for incense. For this reason Hawai'i was known to the Chinese as the "Sandalwood Islands."

At one time the dry forest lay just below the shrub community on the leeward side of Haleakalā. The stunted trees and shrubs are generally widely spaced, and the height of the trees frequently does not exceed 25 feet (8 m). Among the plants found in this forest are halapepe, mamane, and 'a'ali'i, as well as the 'iliahi and the

The bright yellow blossoms of the mamane tree are an important source of food for several native nectar-feeding birds. The mamane grows throughout the park and varies from a height of only a few feet to over 40 feet.

The ʻohiʻa, whose brilliant red blossoms are considered sacred to the Hawaiians' fiery goddess Pele, grows throughout the park. Able to thrive in dry habitats as well as moist ones, the ʻohiʻa is probably Hawaiʻi's most abundant native tree.

***Overleaf:** Early morning light plucks the park's cliffs and cinder cones out of night's obscurity. Photo by Jeff Gnass.*

JEFF GNASS

Slow cooling caused this volcanic cliff to break into unusually regular, square columns. As the rocks break off they scatter themselves among the hardy native species of bunchgrass and pukiawe which manage to live along the volcano slopes.

ubiquitous *'ohi'a*. Vast tracts of these plants were burned and cleared (primarily to create grassland for cattle grazing) but some of the few remaining trees associated with this life zone can be seen along the lower end of the Kaupō trail where it exits the eastern end of the eroded valley. Several other remnants of dry forest remain on the island, although they are quite small in size. Some plant species found in the lower reaches of the dry forest are also found in the coastal strand of vegetation, but most of this lower community has been wholly altered by human activity.

The rain and cloud forests, with their associated high-elevation bogs, are the most densely forested of the plant communities found in Haleakalā. Located over the ridge on the northeastern side of the park and stretching up from the coastal area of the Kīpahulu District, they are difficult to reach and even more difficult to penetrate. These forests of primarily *'ohi'a, koa, 'olapa,* and several species of ferns are almost continuously shrouded by clouds. Constant rain and mist, together with the tangle of trees, vines, ferns, and moss, create an effect wherein you may imagine yourself a solitary traveler in time, transported back to a place remote and primeval, where nature has retained control.

In an eye-catching response to the harmful rays of the sun, the 'ama'u fern has developed red pigmentation in its young, vulnerable fronds. As the fronds mature they gradually assume their normal green color.

The Hāna region of Maui, on the windward side of the island, is characterized by its life-giving abundance of water. Exotic plants such as the philodendron and guava, as well as the less aggressive native plants, grow here in a thick, green profusion.

The forest community of life is very specialized. Endemic tree snails may live out their entire lives on one individual tree, not chewing the leaves but simply cleaning the detritus (organic debris) and algae from the tree's surfaces, allowing the process of photosynthesis to be carried on more efficiently. The forest is home for the crested honeycreeper, an endangered species of forest bird that is entirely dependent on its community of plants. It is also the home of the introduced pig, which forages for roots and churns up the ground so badly that the soil looks as if it has been rototilled. Such erosion-causing activities threaten portions of the forest.

The alpine bogs found above the rain forests are the highest in the state. Trapping much runoff from the surrounding grasslands of these higher elevations, the swampy areas contain a valuable record in the layers of pollen grains that have accumulated over thousands of years. Examination of these pollen records is beginning to reveal information about the early vegetation and climate of the Hawaiian Islands. They may further prove to be the essential link in piecing together the biological history of the Islands.

The alpine zone, elevationally the highest community of plants in the park, is represented on the western-summit region and in small patches of grassland on the eastern half of the volcano rim. On the western side it is almost a desert, with less than 25 inches of rainfall each year. Living conditions are harsh. Intense sunlight, freezing temperatures, and strong winds combine with the low rainfall and porous cinder soils to limit the types and numbers of the plants that are able to exist here. The *'ahinahina* (silversword), *kupaoa*, and spare bunchgrass are the dominant native vegetation types here.

On portions of the eastern half of the volcano rim, the alpine grassland, with its native bunchgrass and *pili* grass, provides a habitat for the migratory American golden plover and the *pueo* (Hawaiian short-eared owl). These small grassland areas are under attack from introduced pigs and goats; destruction of the grassland would surely result in a loss of habitat for dependent birdlife.

The Influence Of People

Beginning with the appearance of the first Polynesian to set foot on Hawai'i's shores and accelerating with the arrival of Europeans, the native ecological balance has been disturbed.

Having evolved in ocean-bound isolation for millions of years, the uniquely Hawaiian flora and fauna became extremely dependent on one another. The difficulty other plants encountered in getting to this environment limited the number of threatening introductions, which through the years made native plants all the more susceptible to foreign arrivals. Thus, a very delicate balance was established in which little margin for tampering was reserved.

The first group of immigrating Polynesians arrived about A.D. 400, bringing with them several familiar food items, among them *kalo, ki,* sugarcane, bananas, bamboo, and coconut, as well as domesticated small pigs and chickens, insects (probably unwanted), and the Polynesian variety of rat.

The initial impact of these first Hawaiians was minimal. They lived in relative harmony with the environment, developing a resource harvesting ethic that restricted their use of certain resources. For example, they immediately replanted shoots of the plants harvested in the wild, and the "bird catchers" took care to release the birds after appropriating their most colorful feathers to use for royal capes. Such common-sense attitudes toward the products of nature ensured the future availability of such items and at the same time contributed to their own survival, an uncontrived but effective plan for renewable resources.

By A.D. 1700, Hawaiians had long since emerged as a distinct Polynesian culture, with language, customs, and a lifestyle all their own. They had also grown from a small band of colonizers to a mighty, populous people. Estimates vary, but some anthropologists believe that by the 18th century, as many as 1,000,000 people may have inhabited the islands. To feed and clothe their population, Hawaiians converted much of the arable land under 1,500 feet (460 meters) elevation into cropland. Dry forest was probably already much reduced, and some native Hawaiian plants and animals heavily impacted.

The seemingly inhospitable cliffs of the volcano are one of the few places in the world that the endangered 'ua'u (dark-rumped petrel) finds suitable for laying its eggs.

It is a matter of conjecture whether or not, had Hawaiians remained isolated in their world, a natural balance would have developed. At any rate, with the European discovery of the islands by Captain James Cook in 1778 and subsequent explorations by La Perouse and by Vancouver, everything changed. On Hawai'i's shores, western influences began to be felt that would alter matters irreversibly. The past two hundred years have seen the rapid introduction of hundreds of

Alien bamboo covers a portion of the slope above Palikea Stream. The aggressive, quick-growing bamboo creates eerie forests so dense that even light is unable to enter them.

alien plant and animal species; the elimination of native species has accelerated proportionally and alarmingly.

Early Hawaiian use of the Haleakalā summit area was minimal. They quarried dense lava rock out of its *pali* for use as adzes and built a large *heiau* on the summit of one of the peaks along its rim. They hunted the dark-rumped petrel *('ua'u)* and the *nēnē* for food. Evidence that they did pass through on foot was left in the stone shelters, platforms, trails, caves, and burial sites that lay within the vast depression and on its outer slopes. The inner volcano was often too cold at the summit to make an overnight stay feasible, and it provided little food. It was essentially a sacred place, visited but not occupied for long periods of time. Unfortunately, there are few Hawaiian artifacts to be found in the volcano, most having been removed by hunters, cowboys, and hikers. Offerings wrapped in leaves are still occasionally found, indicating that local reverence for this large mountain continues into the present.

The first recorded ascent of Haleakalā by Europeans was made on August 21, 1828, by three missionaries. After spending an uncomfortable night on its slopes, the party returned and subsequently described the wonders they had seen to the rest of the world:

> *We beheld the seat of Pele's dreadful reign. We stood on the edge of a tremendous crater, down which, a single misstep would have precipitated us, 1,000 or 1,500 feet. This was once filled with liquid fire, and in it, we counted sixteen extinguished craters.*

Thirteen years later the summit area was explored and again described, this time by members of the United States Exploring Expedition commanded by Charles Wilkes, Lt., U.S.N. They were the first to formally record the mountain's name as Haleakalā, learned from local residents who told them that from certain vantage points on the island the morning sun appeared to rise right out of the volcano! The expedition map of the inner volcano was the first to be published, and it led to a debate over the processes behind its formation.

Early cattle-ranching activities used part of the volcano for grazing land. Cattle were driven down the Sliding Sands Trail to the eastern end of the volcano at Palikū. Left there through the summer, they gradually returned to the outer slopes and remained until the first winter rains. For many years after the park was established, maverick cattle and horses from this early period

GREG VAUGHN

Arriving on the islands as spores which could travel for miles on light winds, ferns are one of Hawai'i's most numerous types of native plants.

GREG VAUGHN

The colors of the pretty koali, a native morning glory, are more subtle than usually conjured in our visions of "island paradise."

PETER FRENCH

A traditional Hawaiian belief holds that those picking ohelo berries along the volcanoes' slopes must first offer some to Pele before eating any themselves.

ED COOPER

Hosmer Grove is the result of an experiment in which North American vegetation—pine, cypress, fir, and cedar—and others, such as the Australian shaggy-barked eucalyptus tree, were introduced for needed watershed and as part of a test to determine whether they could provide a basis for a timber industry in the Islands. These trees were planted alongside native Hawaiian plants, mostly low-lying shrubbery. A walk through the grove is thus a study in contrasts that dramatically illustrates how native plants must struggle in order to survive in the shade of overreaching aliens.

were occasionally found within the volcano. The rock walls along the road to the summit were left from the days when portions of the outer slope were grazed by cattle; the walls were fences to guide the cattle as they were driven up and down the slopes.

Ranching and its use of large tracts of land put increasing pressure on the limited resources of the islands. Many acres were cleared of native forests in order to expand grazing lands. The elimination of these native forests decreased water supplies for agriculture and the growing population of human inhabitants not to mention the associated dependent wildlife. There is some evidence that even local weather was affected by their removal.

As a result, the territory of Hawai'i set up the Board of Agriculture and Forestry and appointed Ralph S. Hosmer in 1904 to the new post of territorial forester. Hosmer's main effort was toward the establishment of forest reserves that would protect damaged watersheds. Fast-growing alien trees were selected over the generally slow-growing native species. Plantings of temperate-zone trees were made on the slopes of Haleakalā as a test to determine whether a timber industry on the Islands would be feasible. The idea was never commercially successful, but the results of the work of Hosmer and others are still seen throughout the Islands. (A grove of trees planted near the entrance to the summit district of the park in 1910 was named in honor of Ralph S. Hosmer in 1954.)

The addition of humans to the ecology of the Hawaiian Islands initiated a slow-building chain of reactions. Human-induced changes in the environment occurred much faster than natural biological changes. Thus humans became the single most important factor in the determination of which plants and animals would survive and which would be lost to the pages of Hawaiian biological history.

Our increasing ability to move about the globe has directly increased the mobility of plants. Human-assisted plants, both noxious and beneficial, have crossed with ease such major geographical barriers as the Pacific Ocean. Once here, in the new and very accommodating Hawaiian environment, these alien plants spread rapidly across the Islands. Taking hold on disturbed land, they meet little resistance from the native vegetation. The best hope for the survival of native species, then, is to maintain undisturbed habitat, minimizing chances for aliens to gain a foothold.

The same sequence of events applies to alien animal invaders. Goats and pigs were introduced by early European explorers for the purpose of providing a source of fresh meat for future visits. This was a good idea at the time, perhaps, but little or no thought was given to the havoc these animals would wreak upon defenseless native vegetation. Nor was the fact considered that no natural predators were present in this new environment to keep their numbers in check. Alien goats, pigs, sheep, and deer browse voraciously on silverswords and other native plants, and cause serious erosion with their sharp hooves. They pose an immediate threat to the survival of many Hawaiian plants. These animals must be controlled if anything of the native biological heritage that remains is to be preserved.

A program to fence the park boundary was completed in 1990 and non-native animals are being removed from the park. With the help of a deputy-ranger program, almost all the alien goats have been removed. As a result, silverswords are already beginning to show signs of recovery.

Other introductions, such as the rat, mongoose, and feral dogs and cats, have brought some native species to the brink of extinction. The ground-nesting *nēnē* was ushered out of existence on Maui by the activities of these introduced predators, helped along by human hunters.

The largest number of known nesting sites for the *'ua'u*, or dark-rumped petrel, an endangered species of sea bird, occurs along the summit cliffs of Haleakalā. A program to trap the petrel's predators—rats and other alien mammals—has succeeded so far in protecting the eggs and young of this bird. Little is known about the *'ua'u*, which lives here from May through October, when it flies off to locations yet to be discovered. The *'ua'u* is found only on Maui, Lana 'i, and Hawai'i.

The living resources of Haleakalā National Park have been inventoried in increasing detail during the past two decades. Priority in park research and management is now given to preserving entire communities and ecosystems rather than focusing on individual species. It is becoming increasingly apparent that native Hawaiian flora and fauna will eventually be lost in areas that are not actively managed for conservation. Alien species will never be eliminated, but careful resource management can successfully preserve native Hawaiian species and communities for the foreseeable future. This is what Haleakalā National Park is all about—a place where a portion of the unique life of the Hawaiian Islands can live on, preserved and protected for the enjoyment and education of people everywhere.

Although supremely suited to the volcano's harsh environment, the silversword is vulnerable to modern pressures from people and alien animals.

ED COOPER

ED COOPER

The land of rainbows and waterfalls one discovers in the Kīpahulu District of Haleakalā is worlds away from the stark land of the summit area desert.

Kīpahulu—A Park Within A Park

Kīpahulu, on the eastern tip of Maui, is set within a classical tropical paradise. Added to the park in 1969, the district has a distinct character of its own. Its lush vegetation and cascading pools of water contrast with the stark summit of the volcano rim to the west. Kīpahulu has seen much use over many decades. Therefore, its history is one that revolves around human occupation and stewardship of the land.

It is not an easy place to reach, for it requires negotiating a rough, narrow, winding road that hugs the cliffs on Maui's windward coast. Snaking in and out of numerous valleys and through dense subtropical vegetation, the road from central Maui takes hours of driving time, although the actual mileage is not great.

This lack of accessibility limits the numbers of visitors, as it did even in ancient times, and until recently has helped preserve the unique character of this region. By escaping the encroachment of civilization, it has become a very special place, one that is being increasingly threatened by outside pressures.

The famous French navigator La Perouse was the first Westerner to describe the Kīpahulu region of Maui. Visiting Hawai'i in 1786, his journal entry for May 20 reads:

> *We beheld water falling in cascades from the mountains, and running in streams to the sea after having watered the habitation of natives, which are so numerous that a space of three or four leagues may be taken for a single village. But all the huts are on the seacoast, and the mountains are so near, that the habitable part of the island appeared to be less than half a league in depth.*

Not quite as populated now, the mountains still rush to the rocky coast, providing only a toehold of habitable ground along the way. Clouds blanket the densely forested mountain slopes above the lowlands in a picturesque scene of tranquillity.

The Setting

Kīpahulu, literally meaning "fetch from exhausted gardens," is but one of three ancient Hawaiian districts that make up the biggest portion of East Maui. The story behind its naming has been lost with the passing of the early individuals who knew it, a situation that is becoming increasingly common as the number of Hawaiian elders diminishes.

Although there were two, more-populated districts to the north and south, Kīpahulu was a significant area to the early Hawaiians. Isolated as it was by difficult overland terrain, unfavor-

Water is the dominant force shaping the Kīpahulu Valley. Heavy rainfall gives life to its people and lush vegetation, swells its streams into cascading chains of waterfalls, and carves the rocks into forms to suit its own designs.

able winds and ocean currents, and a rocky coastline that made shore landings hazardous, its inhabitants enjoyed the benefits of owing little allegiance to outside chiefs. Fishing and the growing of *kalo*, bananas, sweet potatoes, and other food crops on the rich lands enabled the people to make a good living and also supply the needs of the local chief.

The park, in order to perpetuate the use of traditional names, calls the district *Kīpahulu* and the gulch containing the popular and beautiful pools *'Ohe'o*. There are at least two dozen pools along Palikea Stream, and these were undoubtedly used by early residents for a host of recreational as well as practical purposes. The stream is also home to rare aquatic life including the 'o'opu, a unique species of freshwater fish.

Kīpahulu is bounded on the south by the district of Kaupō. Once again, the significance of the name has been lost, but Kaupō translates as "landing place of canoes at night" and may simply describe the calm waters of evening in the normally choppy 'Alenuihaha Channel.

Kaupō once supported a large population and was a place of residence favored by many *ali'i* (chiefs). It was also the district where Nick Soon, an enterprising Chinese storekeeper, made his home near the turn of the century. It was Mr. Soon who introduced much of the modern world to East Maui. His installation of electric lights and his 1916 "Model T"—shipped to Kaupō in pieces and reassembled there—attracted attention and aroused the curiosity of local residents.

Nick Soon was also a meticulous photographer. His pictures have become a most valuable historical record of early Kaupō, and his memory is still respected in the sparsely settled district. The Lo'alo'a Heiau, or temple, is found within the Kaupō District. Now a national historic landmark, the stone platform was used about 1810 by Prince Liholiho, who eventually became King Kamehameha II.

North of Kīpahulu is the district of Hāna. It was here that Queen Ka'ahumanu, the favorite wife of King Kamehameha I, was born. And it was at Hāna that Chief 'Umi a Liloa, of the Big Island, defeated the forces of Maui and claimed it as territory of the island of Hawai'i. The battle to regain the land was a long and bitter struggle, but Hāna was eventually recaptured without a fight by Maui's King Kahekili, when he cut off the water supply to the invader's fortress on Ka'uiki, the large hill beside Hāna Bay. (A few miles northwest of Hāna is Pi'ilanihale, the largest Hawaiian stone structure in the state.)

A sense of tradition colors the Kīpahulu region of Maui, removed as it is from the island's more developed districts. The archaeological wealth of its prehistoric temples and fishing villages attests to the region's importance to the ancient Hawaiians, and many of their cultural practices persist here. One century-old tradition that many modern visitors enjoy is swimming in the pools of Palikea Stream.

JEFF GNASS

The cascading waters of Upper Palikea Falls beckon the eye up the verdant eastern slopes of Haleakalā. Although the first Polynesian inhabitants of the Islands did learn to reap the benefits of this natural richness they also converted it to their own purposes. Archaeological evidence shows that the Islands' first arrivals brought plants such as taro, coconut, and breadfruit carefully packed in their double-hulled canoes. By replacing much of the native vegetation with these crops, these early people were the first of many to alter the original face of Hawai'i.

ED COOPER

Early Hawaiian Life

For Kīpahulu inhabitants, daily activities included farming, fishing, and a variety of chores, including kapa beating, the weaving of mats, canoe building, and the manufacture of household furnishings. Personal adornments were also fashioned; here, as in all of Hawai'i', they reached a greater state of refinement than in the rest of Polynesia. Villages were situated along the coast to take advantage of the level ground, the cool sea breezes, and the accessibility of good fishing grounds.

Fish ponds, located at several points along the coast, trapped and held fish until they were needed. The remains of two such enclosures lie just north of Hamoa Beach. Fresh-water streams such as the Palikea provided *'opae* (a native shrimp) and *'o'opu* (a freshwater goby). Fishing and agriculture continue to supplement the incomes of present-day inhabitants of the district.

The lands within major Hawaiian districts were usually subdivided by the *ali'i* into narrow strips called *ahupua`a*. The ahupua'a usually ran from a narrow *uka* (upland) section to a broad *kai* (sea) or coastal section. Divided in this fashion, each pie-shaped strip of land provided its tenants with all the necessities for living. The upland yielded timber for construction, kapa for cloth, bird feathers for the *ali'i*, and fiber for fish lines and nets. The middle ground was well suited for growing crops, and the coastal area provided fishing and land for villages.

Hawaiians had a name for each of the smaller land divisions. The land on the Hāna side of

ED COOPER

Marshy taro fields checkerboard the Ke'anae Peninsula, on Maui's northeastern coast. Much like rice in Asia and the white potato in northern Europe, taro is the Hawaiian "staff of life," and figures prominently in Hawaiian tradition. It is said that the first-born child of Papa and Wakea, the mother and father of the human race, was born deformed. Papa buried this child and in the night he sprouted roots and emerged as a long stalk, the taro plant. Later, when the first people were born, they were instructed to care for their little brother the taro, so that he might care for them. For hundreds of years taro has been used by Hawaiians, to eat baked or steamed. They also take baked taro rootstock, peel it, pound it into a paste, then mix it with water to create their famous "poi."

ED COOPER

Palikea Stream was called *Papauluana* and the one on the Kaupō side *'Alae Iki*. These names are used infrequently today, having lost their popularity with the passage of time.

The people of each district shared the wealth of their labors through the *'ohana*. Best described as an "extended family," which may include many people not necessarily kin, the individual members of an *'ohana* look out for the well-being of other members. The sharing is done not out of a sense of social obligation but from sincere interest and affection between family members and neighbors. Historically it was headed by a *haku*, in the Western way of thinking a sort of master or "overseer." The *haku* supervised everything from work and worship to family councils and the ceremonies held for visiting *ali'i*. Even though ways of making a living have changed drastically, the *'ohana* is still a vital factor in the Hawaiian way of life and a cohesive force within the Hawaiian ethnic group.

SUGAR

Hawai'i was an independent monarchy when the first raw sugar was produced here in 1802. Sugarcane was planted on lands leased from the king. This land arrangement was satisfactory to everyone, at least until the financial benefits of sugar production in Hawai'i started to increase. Knowledge of the profits to be made in sugar soon prompted a reassessment in the traditional pattern of landholdings, and pressure began to mount for private ownership of Hawaiian land.

The result was the "Great Mahele" of 1848. Initiated under the reign of King Kamehameha III, the Great Mahele changed land-use and ownership concepts throughout Hawai'i. It made land available to the sugar barons and gave rise to large sugar corporations. It apportioned land among chiefs, the government, and the throne. For the first time, commoners had the right to file for title to the lands they occupied. But few did—the legal procedures to obtain land were complex and expensive. Most commoners continued to live on their small parcels, and after the death of the original tenant the land eventually became part of the holdings of the owners—usually the crown or a local chief—of surrounding lands.

Interest in sugar grew rapidly in East Maui. The first plantation was established in Hāna in 1849. Others soon followed. The exact sequence in which lands for the Kīpahulu sugar plantation were consolidated is not known, but little interest was shown by plantation operators in the mar-

ginal land along Palikea Stream. Resident Hawaiians were not evicted from their land; nor, for that matter, were they directly involved in plantation operations. They continued to farm their small parcels for their personal needs, sharing any excess with kinfolk and neighbors.

It cannot be said that the sugar operation in Kīpahulu was a huge success. Beset with problems of transportation, steep slopes bisected by deep gulches, and a dependence on rainfall for irrigation, the mill ceased operations in 1925. It had changed hands several times since it began production in 1881.

During its operation, raw cane was carried to the Kīpahulu mill by several methods. A flume that stretched over ʻOheʻo Gulch carried harvested cane from the Hāna side of the strip to the mill site, which lay farther to the southwest. (The concrete flume towers are still visible on either side of the gulch, but nothing remains now of the V-shaped flume or the narrow walkway that the towers once supported.) Cane was also hauled downhill by mule to the road, where it was carried to the mill in carts, a method whose slowness added to the costs of operation and made the Kīpahulu plantation less competitive.

After the plantation had succumbed to economic pressures and ceased operations, the land was briefly utilized for pineapple production, but this crop also proved to be financially unsuccessful. In 1928 cattle ranching was introduced; it remains the predominant land use in lower Kīpahulu. The old sugar mill site, privately owned, can be easily seen from the road on the Kaupō side of Palikea Stream about one mile from the bridge.

The Upper Kīpahulu Valley

Kīpahulu Valley, the central geologic feature of the district, is six miles long from its headwall (forming the eastern rim of Haleakalā Volcano) to the coast. The lower portion has seen intensive use and alteration by human activities, but the dense upper forest has remained relatively undisturbed. Early Hawaiians rarely ventured into the upper reaches of the valley. In fact, there is little to prove that they actually did enter the areas above 1,800 feet (550 m). Public entry into the upper forest is now strictly prohibited. It has been set aside solely as an ecological preserve, and as such it provides an unparalleled scientific opportunity to understand an entire native Hawaiian rain-forest ecosystem.

Preliminary studies have indicated that the plant community of the forest is about ninety percent native. It also contains at least four rare native birds, including the Maui *nukupu'u*, previously thought to be extinct, the beautiful *'akohekohe* (crested honeycreeper), the Maui parrotbill, and *'akepa*. Nearby, in an adjacent forest, a genus and species of bird previously unknown to science—the *po'ouli* (*Melamprosops phaeosoma*)—was discovered in 1973.

The dense swamps and nearly impenetrable jungle of the upper Kīpahulu Valley will someday undoubtedly yield further discoveries. But even more importantly, the successful preservation of this natural ecosystem will assure that there is at least one place in Hawai'i where native rain forest plants and animals will continue to thrive as free as possible from the impacts and introductions of humankind.

The upper Kīpahulu Valley contains many rare and endangered species of plants and animals and thus presents a rare opportunity to preserve a tract of native vegetation intact. Recognizing the upper valley's immense value to science, as well as its value as a uniquely Hawaiian ecosystem, the park has designated it a "Biological Reserve." In order to preserve this fragile area, entrance into the Reserve is strictly regulated.

Densely packed with impenetrable forest and often completely covered with a blanket of low-lying clouds, the upper Kīpahulu valley still holds many secrets. Perhaps even more precious than the wealth of scientific information it preserves is the mystery it imparts to our world.

Seekers of understanding, scientists continue to carefully probe the secret origins of Hawai'i's unique rain-forest environment. Where did the original plant colonists of these islands come from, and how did they manage to create a flourishing ecosystem? How do the different plants and animals of this natural community interact? These are questions that must be answered if Maui's fragile balance of nature is to be maintained.

Kīpahulu Today

The Kīpahulu District enjoys pleasant subtropical weather nearly the year around. Daytime temperatures seldom exceed 85°F (30°C), and although the humidity is usually high, the prevailing northeast trade winds make the climate quite comfortable. The area receives about 70 inches (180 cm) of rainfall a year, most of it brought inshore by the moisture-laden trades. *Kona* (southerly) winds occasionally bring heavy rains and overcast skies, but the condition usually passes within a few days.

Swimming in the pools of Palikea Stream is a popular activity, but those who are familiar with the area keep an eye on how high the water gets, particularly during times when the upper slopes are receiving heavy rains. The stream can flood quickly, turning its placid waters into a raging torrent, and it has been known to carry swimmers out to sea.

In order to best discover what Kīpahulu has to offer, the area should be entered in the same manner that the Hawaiians did: following the ancient pathways on foot. One upland route leads to the upper pools of Palikea Stream and continues on, winding through dense bamboo forests and jungle-like vegetation, to the base of Waimoku Falls. Another trail winds along the edge of the pasture to an ancient Hawaiian planting area.

Here, until less than a century ago, *kalo*, banana, yams, *ki*, and other traditional crops were grown to support the local residents. Efforts are under way to document the evidence of historic agricultural activity here.

Throwing their silhouettes against the golden curtain of the eastern sky, these hala (pandanus) trees pose like dancers along the coast.

Remnants of the district's early history of habitation are numerous but not always easy to discover. Hidden by thickets of exotic guava and dense underbrush, most of these sites await archaeological investigation. Rock walls, piles of rock, and terraced land may all be significant parts of the early history of the area.

The interesting birdlife frequently observed along the coastal area includes the white-capped noddy (*noio*), frigate bird (*'iwa*), and white-tailed tropic bird (*koa'e kea*). In winter the wandering tattler (*'ulili*), darting among the rocks in the stream, and the golden plover (*kolea*) can be seen.

The Kīpahulu District of Haleakalā National Park was established in two stages. The upper valley, because of its pristine nature and scientific value, became part of the park in 1951. The part containing the lower valley and coastline was added in 1969, largely through the efforts of The Nature Conservancy and private individuals.

The rocky coastline of the Kīpahulu extension of the park completes the continuum of life zones that runs from the volcano rim to the sea. In profile, the park illustrates the story of plant and animal life and the climatic and geographic factors that control their distribution. The diversity of life zones ranges from areas with alpine temperatures and less than 25 inches (63.5 cm) of rainfall per year to dense rain forests where the humidity is nearly a hundred percent. And finally, there is the coastline, with temperatures occasionally exceeding 85°F (30°C), modest rainfall, and heavy trade winds.

Kīpahulu presents an invaluable opportunity to preserve not only a place but a concept of the traditions and moods of old Hawai'i. Although these may be intangible aspects at best, they offer great rewards in learning about and appreciating a people whose love of life and harmony with nature is natural and joyful. It is the hope of many that Kīpahulu and all of East Maui can be preserved for the values that are already there and not those that can be added. Administrators of Haleakalā National Park recognize these aspects in their management approach to the area. They understand that the whole of East Maui . . . its people, culture, lifestyle and history, as well as its natural beauty and unique, fragile ecosystems containing many rare and endangered species of plants and animals . . . is a resource of national significance.

GREG VAUGHN

A visit to Haleakalā's Kīpahulu Valley offers visitors the chance to immerse themselves, not just in Palikea Stream's refreshing waters, but in the unique environment and rich history of this region as well.

SUGGESTED READING

ARIYOSHI, RITA. *Maui On My Mind.* Honolulu: Mutual Publishing of Honolulu, 1985.

DAWS, GAVAN. *Shoal of Time: A History of the Hawaiian Islands.* Honolulu: University of Hawai`i Press, 1974.

DAWS, GAVAN. *Hawaii: The Island of Life.* The Nature Conservancy of Hawaii, 1988.

LAMOUREUX, CHARLES H. *Trailside Plants of Hawai`i's National Parks.* Honolulu: Hawai`i Natural History Association, 1995 (reprint).

MEDEIROS, ARTHUR and LLOYD LOOPE. *Rare Animals and Plants of Haleakala National Park.* Hawai`i Natural History Association, 1994.

STONE, CHARLES AND DANIELLE STONE. *Conservation Biology in Hawai`i.* Manoa: University of Hawai`i, 1989.

Haleakalā Today

Retracing the path of the Hawaiian demigod Māui, increasing numbers of park visitors make the predawn journey to the House of the Sun to wait for the first rays of daylight to steal over the eastern rim of the volcano. Huddled against the cold of the morning air at nearly 10,000 feet (3,000 m), visitors nevertheless enjoy the spectacular play of color on the clouds as the sun nears the horizon. Sometimes the view is obscured by clouds racing the sun to capture and enshroud the summit of the mountain. One wonders if Māui, too, had to contend with nature's capriciousness.

Viewing conditions at the summit of Haleakalā are generally best in the summer and fall months (May through October). Although cloudy, rainy, and even freezing weather can occur at this high elevation at any time of the year, winter and spring months bring a greater abundance of rainfall and, above the 9,000-foot (2,700 m) level, even snow. There have been times when up to 4 feet (1.22 m) have been recorded at the summit of Haleakalā. Frost is not unusual even at 7,000 feet (2,100 m) at park headquarters, which is not quite high enough to count on a snowfall every year but which occasionally has winter dustings that last for several hours.

Wintertime also brings a general easing in the strength and frequency of the prevailing, northeast trade winds. During this slack period, subtropical storms originating in the northwestern Pacific Ocean sweep in from the south, or *kona* direction, bringing thunder, lightning, and high winds. The normally drier southern coasts and lower elevations enjoy the benefit of these kona storms. Winter weather often obscures the inner volcano during the day, but provides sunsets of rare beauty, when the sun slowly slices down through the layers of cotton-like clouds that stretch to the horizon. During the late summer, a tropical depression or, rarely, a full hurricane may approach from Central America.

Haleakalā is a place of changing moods. Much of the feel of Haleakalā comes from the clouds that almost daily ring its slopes. Rising and

JIM MACK

Blossoming only once in its lifetime, the silversword spends itself in a dazzling moment of color and exuberance. Summer visitors to the park can witness this rare display.

Every day pilgrims ascend to the summit of Haleakalā to witness the passion play performed by light and shadow as the sun reappears once again over the eastern horizon. Since this stage is set by the capricious weather of Maui, each dawn offers a unique and unpredictable performance.

WILLIAM WATERFALL

falling in a predictable cycle, these constantly moving clouds lend an aura of dream-like beauty to the volcano's austere dominance over the island. Boiling and seething in slow motion, wisps of moisture occasionally engulf, in an ethereal fog, the twisting road to the summit of the mountain; familiar trees and meadows suddenly seem strange, as if we had entered some mysterious realm. Once above the half-world of the clouds, however, the landscape resumes a docile character.

It is an exhilarating experience to be able to gaze all the way out to the western horizon, with perhaps only the summit of Pu'u Kukui (West Maui) rising out of the mist as if in some storybook kingdom. Mark Twain, in his book *Roughing It*, described his visit to Haleakalā and said of the clouds stealing the view of the checkerboard valley below: *I felt like the Last Man, neglected of the judgment, and left pinnacled in mid-heaven, a forgotten relic of a vanished world.*

The park is at its finest in the morning hours. As the day passes, rising warm air pushes the clouds ever higher, until they start pouring through the Ko'olau and Kaupō gaps into the crater. Once inside the summit depression, the clouds ebb and flow like tides on a beach, occasionally covering the entire valley floor. As evening approaches, the air and land start to cool, and the clouds drain out, sometimes leaving scattered pools or remnants that eventually dissipate. Evening hours also bring shadows that, as they lengthen, creep across the central valley floor, highlighting it as they push the fading sunlight ahead of them. Hues of purple, deep blue, and black contrast sharply with the dying shades of sun-heightened red, yellow, and gold. It is a daily cycle of constant change, and one day is never like any other.

Temperatures at the summit range from 35° to 77° F (2° to 24°C) in the summer and 26° to 75° (-3° to 24° C) in the winter months, and it can be cold, wet, and windy any time of the year. Lows in the teens have been recorded, a far cry from the year-round warmth of the beaches and the swaying palm trees down on Maui's coast.

Haleakalā is primarily a wilderness park. Approximately 32 miles (52 km) of hiking trails criss-cross the vast valley floor, weaving in and out among cinder cones, over jagged lava flows, to the far side of the volcano at Palikū ("Vertical Cliff"). An area that receives at least four times the rainfall of the summit areas, Palikū is lush with the growth of trees and shrubs. A gap in the volcano wall of Palikū allows additional moisture in the form of clouds to condense on the foliage and promote further growth.

Palikū is the site of one of the wilderness cabins constructed by the Civilian Conservation

JOHN I. KJARGAARD

A ghostly image moves among the clouds surrounded by an arcing rainbow, echoing the photographer's movements. The "Brôcken Specter" is the result of a unique combination of clouds and light.

Corps (CCC) in 1937. The cabins provide islands of comfort in the wilderness area and are used heavily by visitors who do not wish to tent camp at the high elevation of the valley floor (6,700 ft/2,040 m). Other cabins are at Kapalaoa, situated on a grass flat at the foot of the southern wall of the inner volcano, and Hōlua, at the base of the 3,000-foot (900 m) Leleiwi Pali on the western end of the inner volcano. Kapalaoa, literally translated, means the whale tooth, and *hōlua* is the Hawaiian word for dryland toboggan. Lying on sleds equipped with wooden runners made from the *mamane* tree, Hawaiians would race down a grassy slope to see which one could go the farthest. According to legend, Madame Pele used the Ko'olau Gap as her *hōlua* when she was in a playful mood. There are also two primitive campgrounds within the wilderness area, one at Hōlua and the second at Palikū. They offer yet another way to experience the park.

Day hikers frequently descend into the volcano via the Sliding Sands Trail and return via the switchbacks on the Halemau'u Trail. On the valley floor, amid the barrenness of the lunar-like landscape, the multi-colored cinder cones take on an entirely new perspective. The piles of cinders tower high above, and the occasional silversword plants that from above looked like blemishes on the slope become studies in stark contrasts—flashes of silver against black or red cinders.

The volcano rim now forms the skyline, and a hiker may have the feeling of walking on the bottom of a giant cup. As afternoon approaches, the clouds, ebbing back and forth through the two great gaps, seem almost to fight with one another, as if in a contest to see which one will dominate the landscape. The whimsical, teasing clouds obscure the vista and shroud the hiker in a world of white mist, occasionally allowing tantalizing peeks at the terrain ahead.

Hiking the park is fun, and the experience far outweighs the effort. A day-long excursion takes one through the Silversword Loop, past Kawilinau (Bottomless Pit) and Pele's Paint Pot. Water and good footwear are necessities for a hike here—and it's a good idea to check at the ranger station for mileages and trail conditions, and for permit regulations.

Overlooks

Pu'u 'Ula'ula (Red Hill), at 10,023 feet (3,055m), is the highest point on Maui. The view from this point can be magnificent, especially when the neighboring islands of Hawai'i, Kao`olawe, Lana`i, Moloka`i, and the tiny, crescent-shaped Molokini are visible. On an exceptionally clear day, even O`ahu can be seen, 130 miles (210 km) away.

Because of the stark, moon-like landscape at Pu'u 'Ula'ula, the domes of Haleakalā Observatories don't seem as surprising as they might in some other setting. Located outside the park boundary, the collection of observatories is operated by several independently owned institutions involved in a variety of solar, lunar, and astronomical research projects. From one, the Lunar Ranging Station, a beam of laser light is bounced off the prisms that were left on the moon by Apollo astronauts. The light makes the earth-moon round trip in two seconds and is an accurate measure of that same distance within 3 inches (7.62 cm). The laser beam is also used to record the northwest movement of the Pacific plate.

Located beside the Haleakalā Visitor Center is "White Hill." A footpath leads to its summit and passes several low, stone-walled circles along the way, the remains of sleeping shelters used by early Hawaiians. Legend relates that Ka'oao, brother of Maui's ruling chief Kekaulike, sought refuge here on the summit of Haleakalā after his men raided Kekaulike's gardens along the coast. The ruling chief pursued his brother back to this location and killed him.

The high vantage point and shelter remnants suggest that Ka'oao may have used this place as a base from which to carry out raids on villages and on unsuspecting travelers who were using the valley as a short cut to Hāna. The area around White Hill became known as Pa Ka'oao (the backyard of Ka'oao) on account of its notorious reputation.

Kalahaku has the longest history of visitor use. In 1894 a small, overnight rock shelter was built here to provide some protection for the adventurous travelers who came on horseback to the volcano rim. The shelter was rebuilt in 1915 and was run by the Chamber of Commerce, which charged a small fee for the use of the iron bunks, mattresses, pillows, and blankets. Prior to the establishment of this facility, early visitors took shelter in caves and behind rock walls. Two such lodgings, Big Flea Cave and Little Flea Cave, were a welcome relief from the occasional cold and windy conditions that prevailed on the mountain. Their names undoubtedly tell us something of the size of the permanent tenants with which human guests had to share accommodations.

Today Kalahaku is noted for the different angle of view it affords of the park and for the collection of silversword plants that lies within a stone-walled exclosure. A rock wall and fence keep visitors from accidentally stepping on young silverswords or compacting the cinders around the mature plants, breaking their shallow roots and eventually killing them.

The small colony of silversword plants at Kalahaku is the largest concentration of the species on the outer western slope, an area so densely covered with silverswords during the late 19th century that they made the hillside look like winter or moonlight.

Leleiwi (literally meaning bone altar) is the first overlook above Park Headquarters. From this vantage point the phenomenon known as the Brôcken Specter is most frequently observed. (The name comes from Brôcken Mountain in the Harz Mountains of eastern Germany, where it was first described.) Conditions must be just right (late-afternoon sunlight and a cloud-filled crater) in order to view this specter, which in actuality is the viewer's own image cast upon the clouds with a rainbow encircling the projected image. Nowadays, when plane travel is so common, this phenomenon is not unusual, since it can be observed from aircraft flying above the clouds.

Cold, wet, windy weather is possible year round in the high elevations of the park. Haleakalā Visitor Center offers sheltered views of the harsh alpine desert landscape found there.

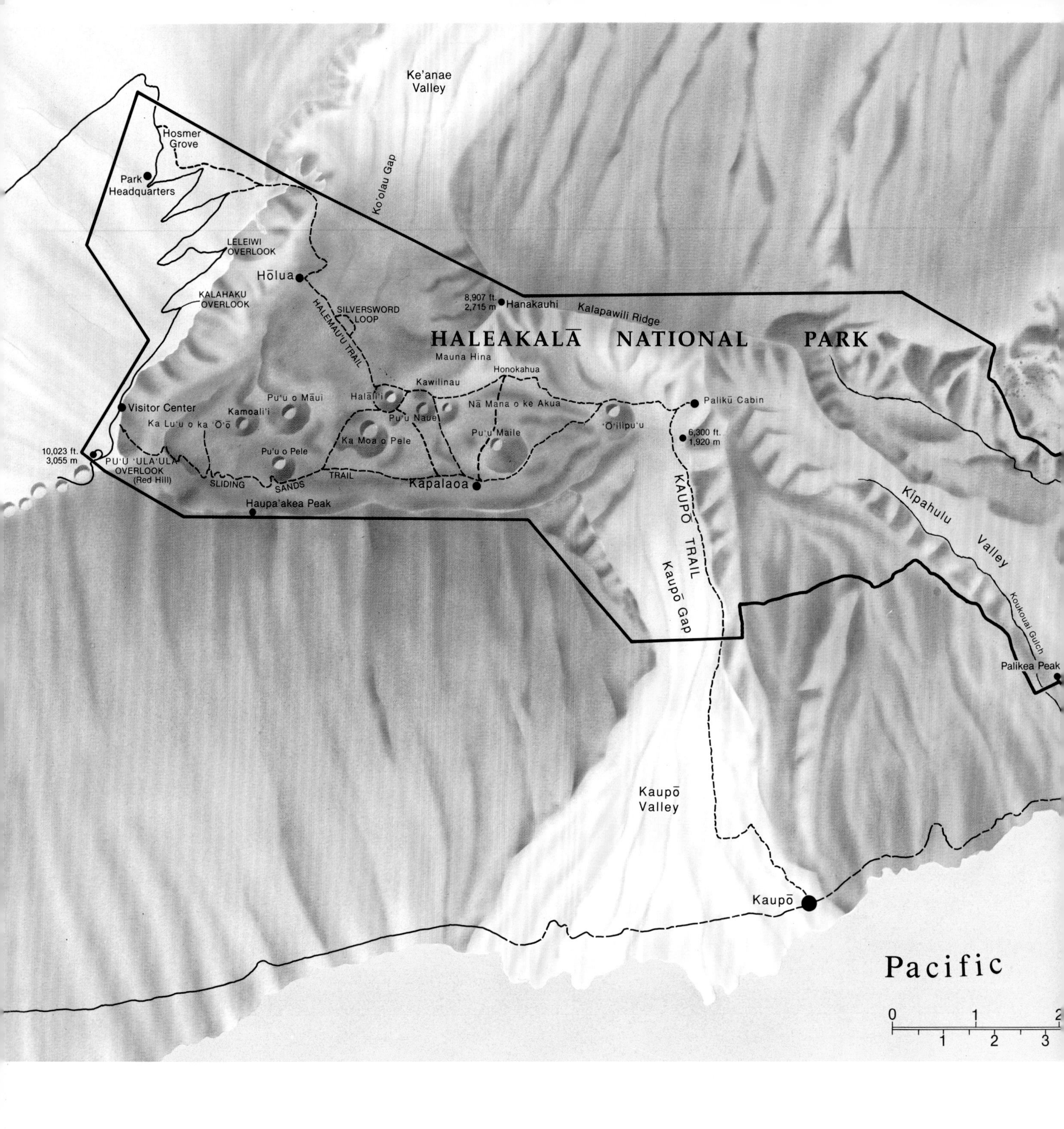

Hosmer Grove

A unique feature of the park is the stand of alien trees known as Hosmer Grove. Among the many species found here are the *deodar* from the Himalayas, the *sugi* from Japan, and the *eucalyptus* of Australia. North America is well represented too, with seven species of pine, as well as cypress, spruce, fir, and others. An easy nature trail extends into the grove for a short distance. Midway through the trail, at the outer edge, several native birds, including the *'apapane, i'iwi* and *'amakihi*, can often be seen feeding on native nectar-producing trees and shrubs such as the *'ohi'a* and *mamane*.

The grove is more than a memorial to a pioneering forester. It reflects the drama of the struggle between native and alien species of plants in Hawai'i. Scattered among the international emissaries of the plant world, native plants compete for available sunlight but make little progress under the covering canopy of the tall aliens. The grove is thus being preserved as a historical enclave in an otherwise predominantly native plant

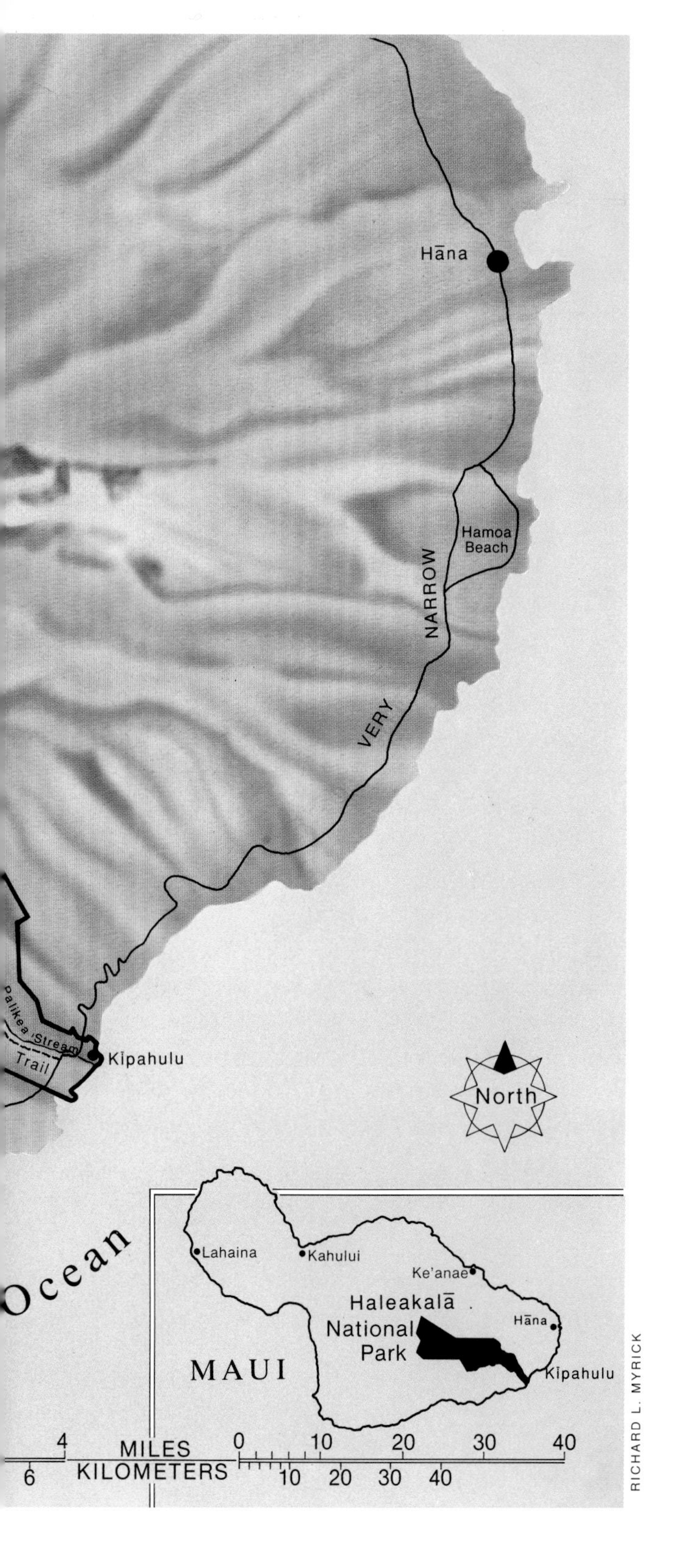

community; it serves as a reminder of the threat that foreign plants pose to native Hawaiian flora and fauna.

On a larger scale, Haleakalā National Park serves a similar purpose. As one of the biologically distinct areas on the island of Maui and in the state of Hawai'i, it preserves one of the largest tracts of relatively undisturbed native vegetation in the state.

Establishing a Park

Haleakalā was initially established in 1916 as the Maui section of Hawai'i National Park. By secretarial order in 1951, a little over 9,000 acres (3,640 hectares) of the Kīpahulu Forest Reserve were added to the unit. Then, on July 1, 1961, Haleakalā was given full status as a separate national park; the Big Island section of what had been Hawai'i National Park became Hawai'i Volcanoes National Park. Since that time the boundary was extended (in 1969) to include the Kīpahulu coastal area. The total park encompasses 28,665 acres (11,605 hectares), much of which has been designated as wilderness under the 1974 Wilderness Act.

This and similar acts of preservation have become very important, not only in Hawai'i, but around the world. Such acts allow the preservation and protection within our national parks of numerous examples of undisturbed ecosystems that provide a reference against which to measure humanity's day-to-day impact on the environment. From these comparisons we can tell if we are breaking the strands that unite plants and animals to each other in the complex and delicate web of life.

Parks also serve as "second-chance" reservoirs from which we can draw information about the interrelationships of life forms that inhabit the earth. They are a place where we may someday reestablish the original balances of nature, gaining opportunities to observe a system of plants and animals that remains undisturbed because it has been preserved. Parks may even eventually prove to be more than just valuable to humankind; they may be *critical*.

It was because of values such as these that in November of 1980, Haleakalā National Park was designated as an International Biosphere Reserve under the United Nations' Man and the Biosphere Program. Haleakalā has also been nominated by UNESCO as a World Heritage Park.

There are many purposes for national parks, aside from the scientific. They undoubtedly contribute immensely to our spiritual refreshment. And from that standpoint, national parks are very popular. Just what is it that brings ever-increasing numbers of people here? Is it the search for solitude? The outdoor experience? Or is it the opportunity to see it the way it *was*—to recapture and relive the excitement of looking out upon an untamed land fresh with the promise of a new beginning, perhaps in much the same way early American pioneers viewed their frontier. If so, this time we are looking at the land with the security of having put something in the bank for the future and not for the promise of untold wealth and uncontrolled development. Seen in this new perspective, national parks are taking on a new importance and a new imperative: protect or destroy.

Haleakalā is a supreme example of the importance of this new imperative. Besides being the unique biological laboratory that it is, it has a special aura unlike any other place in the entire world. The sheer grandeur of Haleakalā's magnificent valley—whether experienced from the footpaths below or in the rarefied air of its high rim—is incomparable.

Reactions to the scene here are many and varied, but it is most often greeted with silence. As we approach the vast depression, we are awed and quieted by thoughts of the immensity of the natural forces that are able to create and destroy, and create again. Even when the scene is partially obscured by clouds, brief glimpses reveal an all-encompassing world that is majestic and profound. For a few fleeting moments, we stand mesmerized by the incredible beauty at our feet, a panorama of sky and clouds and crimson volcano illuminated by the radiance of the sun. It is like standing on the edge of the world not knowing how far is down—and not caring.

ED COOPER

In this portrait (displayed in the park's Haleakalā Visitor's Center) artist Paul Rockwood depicts the dramatic moment when Māui, powerful and mischievous demigod of the Polynesians, battled with the sun atop Haleakalā.

Published by KC Publications, 3245 E. Patrick Ln., Suite A, Las Vegas, NV 89120.

Inside back cover: Colors play across the sky in the rarefied moments before dawn. Photo by William Waterfall.

Back cover: The rare ʻahinahina calls to those wishing to experience a unique type of island beauty. Photo by Ed Cooper.

Created, Designed, and Published in the U.S.A.
Printed by Tien Wah Press (Pte.) Ltd, Singapore